UNPLUG

BREATHE

CREATE

A MONTH OF CREATIVE EMPOWERMENT THROUGH MEDITATION

Unplug Breathe Create: A Month of Creative Empowerment
Through Meditation is a work of my own creation.

The information in this book was correct at the time of publication,
and the Author does not assume any liability for loss or damage
caused by errors or omissions, again, this is my perspective, opinion,
and experience, so it has been written as such.

ISBN - 979-8-9865393-3-1

Cover, Book Design, and Layout by megs thompson, megswrites llc
www.megswrites.com

www.inomniaparatuspublishing.com

"ODD, HOW THE
CREATIVE POWER AT
ONCE BRINGS THE
WHOLE UNIVERSE
TO ORDER."

—VIRGINIA WOOLF

This journal is part of the UNPLUG BREATHE CREATE series & designed to be used alongside a bespoke guided meditation.

Download this month's meditation using the QR code below:

HOW TO BEST USE THIS JOURNAL & MEDITATION

UNPLUG

The first step to reconnecting with ourselves as creative beings is to unplug & disconnect even temporarily from the countless electronic tethers that keep us firmly held in the world of shoulds & must's.

BREATHE

Take a few deep breaths, paying close attention to the way oxygen moves through your mouth & nose, filling your lungs & reawakening the creative genius locked safely within you, exhaling any fears, hesitations, or doubts that may filter your magic.

CREATE

Release your desire to control, plan & perfect every step & movement you make. Embrace the often wild, messy & chaotic magic that comes with allowing your inner creative to explore & play. Prepare yourself to experience fulfillment & satisfaction in new & creative ways.

DAILY ROUTINE

While moving through your day, begin implementing the use of affirmations. Both habits & beliefs are formed & strengthened through consistent repetition & before you know it your thoughts will become truths.

Included below are powerful affirmations that when paired with your daily tasks & activities, will empower you through this month of finding & claiming your own creative space.

I recommend repeating one or more of these affirmations aloud anytime you find yourself in front of a mirror, washing your hands, or refilling your beverage of choice.

I AM CREATIVE.

I AM POWERFUL.

I AM AN AUTHORITY.

30-DAY ENERGY TRACKER

When you've completed your daily meditation, make note of a single word or phrase that best describes your energy level in that moment.

Day 1	Day 2	Day 3	Day 4	Day 5
Day 6	Day 7	Day 8	Day 9	Day 10
Day 11	Day 12	Day 13	Day 14	Day 15
Day 16	Day 17	Day 18	Day 19	Day 20
Day 21	Day 22	Day 23	Day 24	Day 25
Day 26	Day 27	Day 28	Day 29	Day 30

DAY 1

When was the last time you felt creative? Where were you? What were you doing? Who were you with? How can you bring more of this into your daily life?

ON A SCALE OF 1-5 WHAT'S YOUR
CURRENT CREATIVITY LEVEL?

DAY 2

What resistance or fears do you feel around the idea of sharing your creativity with others? Are these feelings based in past experiences or assumptions?

ON A SCALE OF 1-5 WHAT'S YOUR
CURRENT CREATIVITY LEVEL?

DAY 3

What places, people, things, scents, tastes, or memories inspire your creativity? How can you connect with these influences more regularly?

ON A SCALE OF 1-5 WHAT'S YOUR
CURRENT CREATIVITY LEVEL?

DAY 4

What are your favorite forms of creative expression?
This may be words, music, paint, food, dance, clay,
wood, steel, yarn, etc. When was the last time you
took an afternoon to enjoy this creative outlet?

ON A SCALE OF 1-5 WHAT'S YOUR
CURRENT CREATIVITY LEVEL?

DAY 5

How did you most enjoy expressing yourself
creatively as a child? Is that something you might still
enjoy today?

ON A SCALE OF 1-5 WHAT'S YOUR
CURRENT CREATIVITY LEVEL?

DAY 6

How do you define creativity? What does identifying as a creative being mean to you?

_____

_____

_____

_____

_____

_____

_____

_____

_____

_____

_____

_____

_____

_____

_____

_____

ON A SCALE OF 1-5 WHAT'S YOUR
CURRENT CREATIVITY LEVEL?

DAY 7

What creative skills are you most impressed & in awe of? What is it about these forms of creative expression that most impress you? Have you ever tried exploring them yourself?

ON A SCALE OF 1-5 WHAT'S YOUR
CURRENT CREATIVITY LEVEL?

DAY 8

What do you consider to be your unique creative strengths? How would you describe these strengths to others? Are these skills you were taught by someone else or through self-discovery?

_____

_____

_____

_____

_____

_____

_____

_____

_____

_____

_____

_____

_____

_____

_____

_____

_____

_____

ON A SCALE OF 1-5 WHAT'S YOUR
CURRENT CREATIVITY LEVEL?

DAY 9

How do you feel about the idea of writing creatively? Is this a practice you enjoy, something you'd like to explore, or an idea that leaves you feeling anxious?

ON A SCALE OF 1-5 WHAT'S YOUR
CURRENT CREATIVITY LEVEL?

DAY 10

Close your eyes. Take 3 deep breaths & ask yourself, how do I want to explore my creativity today? What answer do you receive? How comfortable are you with trusting your intuition to guide your creativity?

ON A SCALE OF 1-5 WHAT'S YOUR
CURRENT CREATIVITY LEVEL?

DAY 11

When was the last time you created something for fun, without purpose or direction? How did the experience feel? What did you enjoy most about the process? What hesitations did you experience?

ON A SCALE OF 1-5 WHAT'S YOUR
CURRENT CREATIVITY LEVEL?

DAY 12

What creative projects or ideas have you wanted to pursue, but decided against? What reasons have kept you from exploring these projects further? Are they related to cost, experience level, fear, etc?

ON A SCALE OF 1-5 WHAT'S YOUR
CURRENT CREATIVITY LEVEL?

DAY 13

When was the last time you felt stuck or stifled in regard to your creative expression? What was stopping you? Was it an outside force, perceived judgement from others, or your own limiting beliefs?

_____

_____

_____

_____

_____

_____

_____

_____

_____

_____

_____

_____

_____

_____

_____

_____

ON A SCALE OF 1-5 WHAT'S YOUR
CURRENT CREATIVITY LEVEL?

DAY 14

What is one task that you complete every day. This may be something mundane, administrative & without much sparkle. How can you approach this task from a more creative standpoint?

ON A SCALE OF 1-5 WHAT'S YOUR
CURRENT CREATIVITY LEVEL?

DAY 15

What limiting beliefs do you hold when it comes to exploring your own creativity? Where did these beliefs originate?

ON A SCALE OF 1-5 WHAT'S YOUR
CURRENT CREATIVITY LEVEL?

DAY 16

Do you have a space in your home where you feel most creative? A space where you're able to unplug, breathe & create freely? This may be a spare room, a closet with a desk, or a corner near a window. How often do you utilize this space?

_____

_____

_____

_____

_____

_____

_____

_____

_____

_____

_____

_____

_____

_____

ON A SCALE OF 1-5 WHAT'S YOUR
CURRENT CREATIVITY LEVEL?

DAY 17

How often do you allow yourself to embrace your own creativity? What's holding you back from prioritizing this time? As with any habit or skill, consistent repetition strengthens & solidifies your confidence as a creative being. Are you able to set aside 10, 20, or even 30 minutes each day to explore your creativity?

ON A SCALE OF 1-5 WHAT'S YOUR
CURRENT CREATIVITY LEVEL?

DAY 18

Have you ever created a vision or mood board? How about a creative inspiration board? What images, colors, patterns, words, feelings, etc would you include on your board? Why? What is it about these items that inspires you creatively?

_____

_____

_____

_____

_____

_____

_____

_____

_____

_____

_____

_____

_____

_____

_____

_____

_____

ON A SCALE OF 1-5 WHAT'S YOUR
CURRENT CREATIVITY LEVEL?

DAY 19

What is one problem or roadblock that you're experiencing? This may be something small or large. How can you approach this issue from a more creative standpoint?

ON A SCALE OF 1-5 WHAT'S YOUR
CURRENT CREATIVITY LEVEL?

DAY 20

What lights you up? What topics or areas in life are you most passionate about? How do you currently use your creativity in these areas? How might you be able to better tap into your creativity?

_____

_____

_____

_____

_____

_____

_____

_____

_____

_____

_____

_____

_____

_____

_____

_____

ON A SCALE OF 1-5 WHAT'S YOUR
CURRENT CREATIVITY LEVEL?

DAY 21

Reflect on a recently completed project. Something you accomplished successfully & are proud of. How might that project have been even stronger, better, more impactful by utilizing your creativity?

ON A SCALE OF 1-5 WHAT'S YOUR
CURRENT CREATIVITY LEVEL?

DAY 22

How do you best communicate your creative side? Is it with words, actions, music, service, food, or something else? Is this something you explore regularly? Why or why not?

ON A SCALE OF 1-5 WHAT'S YOUR
CURRENT CREATIVITY LEVEL?

DAY 23

Where do you feel the most resistance when it comes to embracing your own creativity? Are these feelings based in past experiences or assumptions?

ON A SCALE OF 1-5 WHAT'S YOUR
CURRENT CREATIVITY LEVEL?

DAY 24

When do you feel the most creatively empowered?

ON A SCALE OF 1-5 WHAT'S YOUR
CURRENT CREATIVITY LEVEL?

DAY 25

What forms of creative expression do you find come most easily, naturally, to you? When do remember first being aware of this ease? How might you apply these same feelings to new forms of creative expression?

_____

_____

_____

_____

_____

_____

_____

_____

_____

_____

_____

_____

_____

_____

ON A SCALE OF 1-5 WHAT'S YOUR
CURRENT CREATIVITY LEVEL?

DAY 26

How would you choose to creatively express yourself today, if time & money weren't factors? What's holding you back from doing so? Is it truly time, money, a fear of failure, or something else?

ON A SCALE OF 1-5 WHAT'S YOUR
CURRENT CREATIVITY LEVEL?

DAY 27

How are you currently communicating your unique voice, message, or story to others? How might you be able to bring more creativity into this process? What feelings or hesitations do you feel around this?

ON A SCALE OF 1-5 WHAT'S YOUR
CURRENT CREATIVITY LEVEL?

DAY 28

How might you introduce yourself to a new
acquaintance in a more creative way? Perhaps
through a short story, a poem, a picture, a graphic, a
song, or something else?

ON A SCALE OF 1-5 WHAT'S YOUR
CURRENT CREATIVITY LEVEL?

DAY 29

What colors, words & images do you feel most represent who you are as an individual, as a creative being, as a business owner, a friend, a partner/spouse/parent?

ON A SCALE OF 1-5 WHAT'S YOUR
CURRENT CREATIVITY LEVEL?

DAY 30

When do you feel most like an authority? Where in your body do you feel this? How would you describe this feeling or sensation? How might you be able to creatively amplify this feeling of authority?

ON A SCALE OF 1-5 WHAT'S YOUR
CURRENT CREATIVITY LEVEL?

If you already have an
UNPLUG BREATHE CREATE
subscription, keep an eye on your
mailbox for your next delivery.

If you aren't yet a member but
would like to be, or are
interested in gifting a
membership to someone else,
scan the QR code below.

www.ingramcontent.com/pod-product-compliance
Lightning Source LLC
Chambersburg PA
CBHW070448130626
46553CB00006B/2313

* 9 7 9 8 9 8 6 5 3 9 3 3 1 *